DOG FINDS LOST DOLPHINS!

And More True Stories of Amazing Animal Heroes

Since 1888, the National Geographic Society has funded more than 12,000 research, exploration, and preservation projects around the world. The Society receives funds from National Geographic Partners, LLC, funded in part by your purchase. A portion of the proceeds from this book supports this vital work.

For more information, please visit www.natgeo.com/info, call 1-800-647-5463, or write to the following address:
National Geographic Partners, LLC
1145 17th Street N.W.
Washington, D.C. 20036-4688 U.S.A.

Visit us online at nationalgeographic.com/books

For librarians and teachers: ngchildrensbooks.org

National Geographic supports K–12 educators with ELA Common Core Resources. Visit natgeoed.org/commoncore for more information.

More for kids from National Geographic:
kids.nationalgeographic.com

For information about special discounts for bulk purchases, please contact National Geographic Books Special Sales:
ngspecsales@ngs.org

For rights or permissions inquiries, please contact National Geographic Books Subsidiary Rights: ngbookrights@ngs.org

Trade paperback
ISBN: 978-1-4263-1031-7
Reinforced library edition
ISBN: 978-1-4263-1032-4

Printed in the United States of America
16/WOR/5

Table of CONTENTS

CLOUD: Dolphin Rescue Dog   4

   Chapter 1: Call for Help   6

   Chapter 2: Rescuer in Training   16

   Chapter 3: Dolphin Duty   26

KASEY: Monkey Miracle Worker   36

   Chapter 1: A Life Changed   38

   Chapter 2: Monkey College   48

   Chapter 3: Miracle Monkey   58

RATS: Heroes in Small Packages   68

   Chapter 1: Hidden Talent   70

   Chapter 2: An Explosive Problem   80

   Chapter 3: Rats to the Rescue   90

DON'T MISS!   101

Index and Further Information   110

CLOUD:
DOLPHIN
RESCUE DOG

Cloud was the first dog to be trained to rescue dolphins.

Scientists do not always know why dolphins and whales get stranded.

When Chris Blankenship got an emergency call to report to the beach, he expected it to be busy. And it was!

About 80 dolphins were wriggling and squeaking in the shallow water. A small army of people worked quickly to help them. Team leaders barked orders. Volunteers put on wet suits for their turn in the water. News reporters were there too. They were looking for a big story.

Chris is a dolphin expert. He has seen dolphins and whales stuck on shore before. This time was different. Usually one or two dolphins get stuck in shallow water. Sometimes they get stuck in the twisty roots of mangrove trees. *But 80 dolphins!* Chris thought. *With so many, how do we know that we've found them all?*

Every time a dolphin or whale gets stranded, it is a race against time. The sooner the dolphins are found, the easier it can be to save them. Chris ran his hands over a dolphin's smooth, rubbery skin. He thought how odd it was that such a good swimmer needed help.

Dolphins are perfect for the underwater world. With their strong bodies and sleek fins, they can swim seven times faster than humans. They can hold their breath for more than 15 minutes and dive 2,000 feet (610 m) underwater.

Dolphins are also very smart. They hunt in groups. They make up games to play. They even name themselves using whistling sounds. Many researchers spend their lives learning how dolphins communicate. In a dolphin's world, every click, whistle, and gesture has a meaning.

Yet sometimes dolphins end up in trouble. They can get stuck on a beach. It's a dangerous situation for them. By the time they are found, most stranded dolphins are sick or have died already.

Why would such smart animals swim so close to a beach? We don't really know. Maybe some stranded dolphins have been sick. Maybe pollution in the water confused them. Maybe they got lost during a storm at sea.

In order to find the answer, scientists study stranded dolphins as they try to help them. They look for clues that will help them keep dolphins safe.

Chris and the animal doctors got to work on the stranded dolphins. The first step: Make sure the dolphin can breathe. Dolphins are mammals, like humans. They have lungs and need to breathe air. They take in air through a blowhole on their back, behind their head.

The stranded dolphins were very tired. They couldn't stay up on their bellies or swim on their own. People took turns holding the animals up so they could breathe. They rested the dolphins on their knees to keep their blowholes above water.

The volunteers also kept the dolphins' skin moist by splashing water on their bodies. A dolphin's exposed skin can dry out quickly in the hot Florida sun.

A team examined each dolphin. They had to find out which dolphins were healthy enough to survive in the wild. The healthiest dolphins were helped back to deeper water right away. Sick dolphins were taken to a special hospital. There they were given medicine and food.

Dolphins and Whales

All dolphins and whales are in the same family—a group of animals called cetaceans (SE-TAY-SHUNS). There are more than 80 different types of cetaceans. The common name for the whole cetacean group is "whales."

Whales are divided into two groups:

BALEEN WHALES

TOOTHED WHALES

Dolphins have teeth, so they are part of the toothed whale group.

	Baleen Whales	**Toothed Whales**
How They Eat	Baleen (BAY-LEEN) whales have comb-like filters in their mouths. They suck in a ton of water and then strain it through the filters.	Toothed whales have a mouth full of shovel-like teeth so they can chew their prey.
What They Eat	Baleen whales eat tiny creatures called krill and plankton that get trapped in their mouths when all of the water filters out.	Toothed whales eat fish, seals, and squid, and some of the bigger whales might eat another whale.
Who They Are	humpback whales, blue whales, and bowhead whales	dolphins, killer whales, pilot whales

Chris popped a fish stuffed with medicine in a dolphin's mouth.

This one is in rough shape, but it seems like a fighter, he thought. Suddenly, a shout got Chris's attention.

"Chris!" yelled a volunteer. "Quick! Come over here!"

Chris ran down the beach to a spot full of mangrove trees. A small group of dolphins were stuck in the trees' thick roots. They must have been separated from the main group. Now it was too late. They were too sick to save.

Chris sighed. *I wish we had some way of locating dolphins. Then we could get to them sooner.*

After that day, Chris kept thinking about what he had seen. He wondered if there was a better way to find lost dolphins. Then Chris started reading about some dogs that worked nearby. They were trained to search for people who get lost on or near the water. The dogs worked along beaches or from boats in the water. They sniffed the air for the missing person's smell. They could even smell objects that were slightly underwater.

Chris wondered: *If dogs can find humans in the water, can they find dolphins too?*

Chris called Beth Smart, the head of the Dolphin and Marine Medical Research Foundation. Beth listened carefully. She liked the idea. Sure, no one had ever used a dog to find beached dolphins or whales. But that didn't mean it was impossible.

Beth agreed to work with Chris on the project. "Let's look for a dog!" she said.

One of Cloud's trainers, Beth Smart, helps sick dolphins recover so they can return to life in the wild.

Chapter 2

RESCUER IN TRAINING

There are many different types of dogs. Beth's first job was to figure out what kind of dog they should get.

Beth and Chris needed a dog that was smart. Not every dog could learn to find dolphins. They needed a dog that could swim well. A good swimmer would be safe working in a boat. The dog needed to be friendly and loyal to its handler. Like most dogs, it had to have a great sense of smell. But most important of all, it must love to play. Looking for lost dolphins is like a doggy version of hide-and-seek. The dog would do its best work when it was having fun.

Chris and Beth heard about a smart puppy from a man who trained police dogs. The pup was a Labrador retriever, a kind of dog that is perfect for working around water. They have webbed paws that help them swim. Labs also have an oily coat that keeps them warm and dry. Beth might have found the perfect pup.

But there was one problem. This puppy was a black bundle of fur. Black is the worst color for staying cool in the hot sun. And boy, does it get hot in Florida!

Beth and Chris decided to try her anyway. The puppy, named Cloud, wagged her tail and yipped with delight when she met them. She licked their hands and walked away. She found a nice big tree and curled up beneath it. *Ha!* Chris laughed to himself. *She is already good at finding shade!*

Beth and Chris knew that Cloud needed to be trained to do as she is told before she learned to find dolphins. They called Mike Clark, the owner of a police dog–training facility. Mike had trained lots of dogs, but never one who searched for dolphins. This was going to be fun!

> **Did You Know?**
>
> **Labrador retrievers are named for the place they came from. They helped fishermen on their boats in the Labrador Sea.**

First, Mike had to start with the basics: doggy manners. Cloud learned to sit, stay, and come when called. She practiced walking next to her handler's side while on a leash. She learned to pay attention to Chris and Mike when they gave her commands.

Soon Cloud had learned the basics. She was ready to start learning how to find scents. This type of training makes use of a dog's sniffing superpowers.

A dog's sense of smell works just like a human's. When a dog sniffs the air, tiny bits of odors enter its nose. In the nose, special cells take in the tiny bits. These cells send signals to the brain. Then the brain tells the dog what the smells are.

Dogs have about 220 million of these special cells. That's 40 times more than humans have. Not only that, but the special place in a dog's brain that is used to decode smells is almost twice as large as it is in humans. Scientists think that this means dogs are 1,000 to 10,000 times better at sorting out scents than people are. They get much more information from a whiff of air than people do.

Beth and Chris collected samples of smells from live dolphins. They put the samples on cotton pads. They placed the pads in tubes. Mike let Cloud sniff the tubes. Then he hid the tubes and asked Cloud to find them. Cloud found the tubes by following the trail of their smell. Mike trained her to sit and bark when she found one of the tubes.

"Good girl! That's right, Cloud!" Mike

and Chris praised Cloud for a successful search. Then they gave Cloud one of her favorite treats: lamb and rice doggy biscuits. Cloud gobbled them up.

After a hard day of training, Chris took Cloud for a walk and a game of fetch. At first, Chris tossed tennis balls for Cloud to bring back. Whenever a palm tree was nearby, Cloud trotted back with a coconut instead. Chris laughed. Cloud sure had a knack for finding things!

But Cloud wasn't the only one learning new tricks. Mike taught Chris how to be a good handler for Cloud. A handler's job is to tell the dog what to do and to keep it under control. Chris had to learn hand signals and voice commands. He also keeps the dog safe from danger.

Working Dogs

Dogs make great pets. They are playful, smart, and loving. But many dogs do more than chase balls and snooze under the table. Working dogs do important jobs all over the world.

Avalanche rescue dogs sniff out skiers buried under piles of snow. Police and airports use dogs to sniff for bombs. Other dogs find drugs or rare animals that criminals might be hiding. Guide dogs help people who have trouble seeing get through their busy days.

Finally, Chris had to make sure that Cloud was in the best spot for finding dolphins. It took a lot of practice, but Chris and Cloud were getting better and better every day.

Chris and Cloud went out every day using blood samples from a few kinds of dolphins and whales. They didn't have samples from every kind. But dolphins and whales come from the same family of animals, so Chris felt sure that Cloud could find any type.

After training, Cloud had to pass a test to show she knew how to do her job. She had to show she could follow commands and sniff out smells—on land and in the water. She also had to prove she could behave. Chris was being tested, too. He had to show that he could control Cloud.

The pair passed their final test with ease. Cloud could find the tiniest drop of hidden dolphin scent. Now Chris and Cloud were an official K-9 unit. They could start working. K-9 is the name given to a team made up of a person and a dog. "K-9" sounds like the word "canine," which means dog.

To celebrate, Chris got Cloud a bright orange life vest. It said, "Working Dog. DO NOT PET." Chris didn't want people to mess up her search by distracting her while she was on the job. Chris put the vest on Cloud. She stood proudly and wagged her tail. Now, Cloud was ready to use her remarkable nose to search for dolphins in trouble.

Cloud greets these two dolphins like they are old friends.

Chapter 3

DOLPHIN DUTY

One day Chris gets a call about a possible dolphin stranding. He wakes Cloud from her spot on the porch. He pulls out her orange life vest. Cloud can barely contain herself. She lets out a bark of excitement. Her tail wags wildly. It's like she's saying, "Hurry up! Let's find some dolphins!"

Chris stops to check that they have all their safety gear. They carry life vests, just in case. They have a device that helps them tell where they are and where they are going.

Cloud and Chris can only search for dolphins in waters deep enough for boats. This rule is for Cloud's safety. If the water is too shallow, a boat might get stuck. And finding dolphins by swimming around or running along the beach would be too tiring for Cloud. Also, stranded dolphins are often sick. Cloud could get sick too if she comes too close to one.

Cloud and Chris head for the dock. It's nearly sunset. Soon the moon and the stars will be the only lights in the sky. *This is why we need Cloud,* Chris thinks. *It would be way too hard to see dolphins in the dark.*

Cloud takes her position in the front of the boat. It's 16 feet (4.9 m) long and sits low in the water so Cloud has a good sniffing spot. The boat is named *Cloud's Waterwings*. Cloud stands and sniffs the air. Her nose wriggles constantly. The salty wind ruffles her black coat.

Chris steers the boat toward the spot where someone had reported seeing a beached dolphin. He knows there might not really be a dolphin there. Reports like these are often mistakes. Sometimes what people think is a dolphin is really a pile of garbage or a clump of seaweed. Still, every call must be checked out.

Chris puts Cloud on alert. That means he tells Cloud to sniff just for dolphins and whales. She knows to signal if she smells one. At first, Cloud stands silently. Chris wonders if the report was a mistake.

Suddenly, Cloud starts to bark. She sits, just as she was trained to do. This is Cloud's signal. She smells a dolphin.

Then Chris sees it! A dolphin lies on the beach ahead. Chris calls for help. When a stranded dolphin is found, experts always come to the rescue. They can take the dolphin to the special hospital if it is sick. They can get it out to sea if it is well. If there are a lot of stranded dolphins, they can gather volunteers to watch over the dolphins until they can sort things out.

There's a chance the dolphin has already died. Even so, it is good that Cloud found it. Scientists can study the body. They can see if the dolphin had any diseases. They can find out what it ate, how long it lived, and how many calves, or babies, it had. They can also tell if pollution hurt the dolphin or if it had ever been hit by a ship or caught in fishing gear.

By learning information about a dolphin that didn't survive being stranded, experts might be able to prevent strandings from happening again. If they can figure out the problem, they can try to fix it.

Did You Know?

Dolphins don't drink water. They get all the water they need from the fish they eat.

Chris steers the boat closer to get a better look at the dolphin on the beach. It's alive, but shark bites cover its body. It needs help fast! Even though the dolphin's condition isn't good, Chris praises Cloud. He gives her a treat. She did her job perfectly. Soon the team of experts arrives. They take care of the injured dolphin. Cloud and Chris hurry back to the dock.

Cloud has found six dolphins and whales in trouble. She once even smelled a stranded pilot whale from half a mile away!

Since Cloud has been such a success, Chris and Beth are planning to put more dogs through the training program. Two German shepherds will follow in Cloud's paw prints. Beth plans to provide dogs to people who look for stranded dolphins and whales in other places, too. Many organizations have shown an interest in having a dolphin-finding dog of their own.

Beth is also thinking about other animals that dogs could help rescue.

Whale of a Job

Cloud might be the world's first dolphin search and rescue dog. But she's not the only pup to lend whales a helping paw.

Scientists at the New England Aquarium have been studying right whales. The easiest way to study them is to collect the whales' scat, or poop. The stinky stuff floats on the top of the water for about an hour before sinking. That's where Fargo and Bob come in. These dogs are trained to ride in research boats. They bark when they smell whale poop. Thanks to these dogs, scientists are learning more every day!

Manatees and sea turtles can get stuck on beaches too. Could dogs be trained to help those animals? Beth thinks so. But it would be too confusing for one dog to learn multiple animal smells. So for now, Beth and Chris are working just on dolphin and whale rescue.

Chris hopes that his new dogs will be natural friends to dolphins like Cloud is. He remembers the day of Cloud's final lesson. Chris took Cloud to a marine park so she could learn the difference between sick and healthy dolphins.

"Where are the dolphins, Cloud?" asked Chris.

Cloud ran to the dock and sat down. Two dolphins popped up from the water. Cloud, with her pink tongue dangling, leaned in for a kiss. It was almost like the dolphins knew that Cloud was their friend.

The dolphins followed Cloud's every move. As Cloud walked up the dock, they swam along beside her in the water. When she turned back, they were still right beside her. And Cloud seemed as interested in the dolphins as they were in her. She stayed and watched them play for hours.

Chris grinned. "If I were to leave you alone, you might move right in with them!" he teased. One thing is certain: Man's best friend has room in her heart for dolphins too.

Kasey helps Ned unscrew the cap from a water bottle. They make a great team.

KASEY: MONKEY MIRACLE WORKER

Ned's life changed forever when he injured his spinal cord in a car accident.

Chapter 1

A LIFE CHANGED

The day that changed Ned Sullivan's life started like any other. Ned was a college student in Arizona. He worked at a big sports magazine. It was the perfect job for a sports fan. Ned got good grades and was looking forward to one day working in sports full-time. Then, in the blink of an eye, his world changed. Ned was in a car accident.

An ambulance came and rushed Ned to the hospital. Doctors saw that his brain and spine were badly hurt. They were very worried.

Doctors called Ned's family, who lived across the country. His mom, Ellen, came right away. She wanted to help him get better. Ned needed to be around family. The doctors said the best hope was for Ellen and Ned to fly back across the country to Boston, Massachusetts, where his family lived.

Ellen and Ned made the trip on a special plane that has equipment for medical emergencies. The flight went well. Ned was home where he needed to be, but he was still in bad shape.

Ned needed the help of a machine just

to breathe. He couldn't move, talk, eat, or drink. The only way Ned could communicate was by blinking his eyes.

The doctors got Ned a spelling board. The board lists the letters of the alphabet. Ellen would touch the letters. When she touched the letter Ned wanted, he would blink. Then they would find the next letter in the same way. Slowly, the words built a sentence.

Ned could tell people what he needed using the letter board, but it took a long time. He asked his mom for more help.

Ned worked hard to get better. But his doctors still worried that he might never speak or breathe on his own again. They told this to Ned and his family. Then one day something amazing happened. Ned started breathing on his own.

It's a miracle! Ellen thought. *If he can learn to breathe again, might he be able to do other things some day?*

The doctors were also excited to see what else Ned could do. Ned's family took him to a special hospital. Many experts on these types of injuries worked there. Plus, the hospital had all the right equipment to help Ned with his treatment.

At the new hospital, Ned had to work harder than he ever had. Ned tried to learn how to speak again. He practiced trying to move his arms and legs. He learned how to control a special wheelchair by sipping and puffing into a straw.

Ned had to relearn how to do things that most people don't think about when they do them, like getting out of bed, dressing, bathing, and eating. He had to do them without using his arms or legs. Ned's progress was slow and difficult. But sometimes, a breakthrough would happen.

"Hi, Mom," Ned cheerfully said one day after months of silence. Ned's voice didn't sound the same. His words came out slowly. Ned didn't like that, but his Mom didn't care. She cheered with joy. *Ned could talk again!* Soon after that, Ned could swallow soft foods. Then he could move his hand a little bit. Ned was finally starting to get better.

After almost a year in hospitals, Ned's doctors said he was ready to go home. This made Ned's mom very nervous.

What if he needs me but I'm not in the

room? she thought. *How will I be able to care for him?*

Ned's doctors had an idea. They suggested he get a helper at home.

What can a helper do for me that my mom can't? Ned thought. But the doctors weren't talking about another person. They were talking about a dog!

There are places that carefully train dogs to do things for people who need help. The dogs can open doors and fetch things for them. This might be just the answer for Ned! But Ned didn't like this idea. He told his Mom he didn't want another dog. His family already had two goofy mutts at home.

"We have dogs," Ned said.

Ned's mom accepted his answer.

Staying Safe

Things like biking, diving, and playing on a playground can be great exercise and lots of fun. That's important for your health. But it's also important to remember to use the right safety gear and follow the rules. Most spinal cord injuries occur in people between the ages of 16 and 26. Risky things like running around the pool, diving into shallow water, and biking without a helmet are often to blame. You can lower your risk by knowing what to do. Follow playground and pool rules. Always wear a helmet when you bike or skateboard.

But she still worried about him. She thought that Ned might need some cheering up. He had made great progress in getting better. Still, all of his hard work did not seem to make him much happier. Then Ellen had an idea.

"Hey, Ned, didn't we once see something on the news about trained monkeys?"

Ned shot her a look.

"I'm serious. Remember? Maybe we could look into that."

Ned wasn't buying it.

The very next day, Ned's sisters, Maddie and Anna, went to an assembly at their school. The topic was safety. The students learned about safe habits, like wearing helmets and seat belts. There was a special guest: a working monkey named Ayla. She was trained to help people who couldn't do things for themselves.

Maddie and Anna rushed home to tell their mom and Ned about Ayla. Ellen couldn't believe it. She had seen something about monkey helpers. Could this be the answer they were looking for?

Ned didn't want to get his hopes too high.

"Maybe," he said.

Did You Know?

The first trained helper monkey went to work in 1979.

Kasey when she was just a baby. She had to wait 15 years until she could attend monkey college.

School was easy for Kasey. She sped through her lessons with ease. Plus she was friendly with all the other students and with the teachers, too. But Kasey wasn't a regular school kid. She was a monkey. And her school was called Monkey College.

Monkey College trains capuchin (sounds like KAH-POO-CHIN) monkeys to help people. It is run by a group called Helping Hands. The capuchin monkeys have perfect fingers and toes for using tools and holding things. They can unscrew the cap of a water bottle, put a disc in a DVD player, and flip a light switch.

Kasey had gone to school for three years. She could pick up and return dropped objects. She could turn the pages of a book. She could even scratch an itch. She was the perfect helper for someone who couldn't use his or her arms and legs. Someone like Ned.

Just like a child, Kasey started learning even before she started school. When she was young, she lived with a human family. There, Kasey got used to the noises and activities that are a part of living with people. This is a very important step in becoming a service monkey.

Around age 15, Kasey was ready to go to college. Like human students, Monkey College students must pass from one grade to the next. Each grade is a little bit harder than the one before.

Kasey's first classroom was a plain room called the Cubicle. Here Kasey learned to copy her teacher. "Monkey see, monkey do" was the name of the game. Kasey earned a tasty treat every time she did exactly what the teacher did.

Megan Talbert was one of Kasey's teachers. She used a baby toy for one of Kasey's lessons. Talbert put plastic rings on a small post. They looked like colored doughnuts. Kasey watched what Megan did. Now, it was her turn. Kasey slid the rings down the post just like her teacher. Megan gave Kasey a spoon of peanut butter. It's one of her favorite foods and served as a reward. "Nice work, Kasey!"

After about a year, Kasey moved to the B Room. Megan went with her. Here, Megan sat in a wheelchair to get Kasey used to it. She did jobs, like pouring a glass of juice, step by step. Kasey learned each step. Then she learned to put all the steps together. Megan also taught Kasey to follow a light pointer. Someone who couldn't point with her fingers could point at something by holding the pointer in her mouth. Then Kasey could get the object the light pointed to and bring it back to the person.

After a year of lessons in the B Room, Kasey was ready for the highest level. It's called the Apartment. This classroom looks like a home. It's an important step in monkey training because it's like the homes where the monkeys will be sent to work.

Kasey and her classmates loved it. They wanted to open all the doors. They wanted to climb all the shelves. They wanted to search through drawers.

Did You Know?

Capuchins are one of the smartest monkeys. They have the ability to use tools and learn new skills more quickly than most other monkeys.

All of the monkeys were allowed time to play and explore. But they had to learn what was a toy and what was not. They had to learn when it was time to work and when it was time to play. They also had to be potty trained.

In the Apartment, Kasey learned to help people by being their arms and legs. She learned how to wash a person's face and scratch itches. She pushed up eyeglasses when they slipped down Megan's nose. She put Megan's hand on the wheelchair's armrest when it fell off. Now, Kasey was a true helper monkey. She was done with school, but there was one important thing left: Kasey needed a person to help.

Megan got a letter from Ellen. She asked Helping Hands for a helper monkey for Ned. The letter said that Ned was part of a big family in a busy home. There were two young girls and two dogs that barked a lot. Older, college-age children were always coming and going. All those things could scare a monkey.

There were good things too. Ned was a young man. He could make friends with a monkey and stay friends for life. Ellen would be home all day. She could help take care of a monkey. The most important thing was that Ned was a hard worker. He put a lot of effort into learning to talk better. Learning to move his arms and legs was difficult, but he tried hard. He never missed a doctor's appointment. Ned was a person who would be very thankful for a monkey's help.

Megan decided Ned should have a monkey. Then she had to choose which monkey would be best for Ned. Like people, monkeys have different personalities. Some monkeys are quiet and calm. Some monkeys are shy. Kasey was bossy, but she was also very friendly and outgoing. Kasey would like Ned and Ellen's busy home.

Megan took Kasey to Ned's home. Then she spent a week teaching the family how to care for Kasey. Megan helped them set up Kasey's cage in Ned's room. She gave them all of Kasey's toys. Kasey's favorite was a black coin purse that zipped open and shut. Megan showed Ellen how to make Kasey's meals: monkey chow, seven times a day.

Finally, it was time for Kasey and Ned to begin working together. Everyone was excited. It was time for Ned to see what Kasey could do.

Calling All Capuchins

Monkey College teaches only capuchin monkeys. Capuchins are very smart. They weigh just six to nine pounds (3 to 4 kg). They are so small they can hitch a ride on a wheelchair.

Capuchins are part of the family of animals called primates. This family includes apes, humans, and all monkeys. Capuchins come from South America. They live for about 40 years. That's four times as long as a dog. A helper monkey can stay with someone much longer than a dog can.

Kasey has helped Ned recover far beyond what anyone imagined.

Chapter 3

MIRACLE MONKEY

"Kasey, come. Sit," Ned asked. Kasey gave Ned a bored look. She hopped up on the coffee table to flip through a magazine instead.

Ned felt sad. *Why doesn't she like me,* he thought.

Before Kasey arrived, Ned and his family couldn't wait to meet her. They thought it would be like getting a new puppy. They thought

Kasey would jump into their arms. They thought she'd hug them and kiss them, and they would all love each other right away.

But the family was forgetting one important thing. Monkeys aren't like dogs. They're more like people. Imagine walking into a house full of strangers. You wouldn't be everyone's friend right away. You would take your time getting to know everyone.

Monkeys are the same way. They watch people. They study how people act. Kasey needed time to get used to her new home. Megan had seen this happen many times. She asked Ned to be patient.

"She'll come around, Ned. Let's try it again, with peanut butter this time."

Megan attached a holder for peanut butter to Ned's wheelchair. Ned could

Did You Know?

Capuchin monkeys can jump 9 feet (2.7 m) from one branch to the next.

bend his finger just a little. That way he could scoop the peanut butter and give it to Kasey.

With a peanut butter prize, Kasey obeyed. She leaped into Ned's lap and licked her sticky reward. But seconds later, she was back on Megan's shoulder.

"It will take time to make friends with Kasey," Megan told him again.

Kasey wasn't always doing what Ned told her to do. But Ned still couldn't take his eyes off her. She played with her toys. She flipped through a book. She zipped and unzipped her purse. At meals, she twirled with excitement, her black fur puffing up.

Having a monkey is a lot of work.

Feeding, washing, and cleaning up after Kasey was hard for Ned's mom. *This is like having a three-year-old with five arms!* Ellen thought.

Slowly Kasey started to feel at home. She helped Ned more and more. She would get Ned a bottle of water, put a straw in it, and hold it to his mouth. She fetched things quickly. She stayed on his lap after gobbling her peanut butter.

One day, Ned's arm slipped off the wheelchair armrest. Kasey hurried over to put it back without being asked. Another day, Kasey dragged a notepad and pencil onto Ned's lap. She loved to doodle. When she was finished drawing, she put the pencil in Ned's hand. It was like she was saying, *Now it's your turn.*

Soon Kasey was watching Ned just as closely as he was watching her. Kasey learned how much Ned could move. When Ned asked her to get the television remote, she brought it back and held it slightly out of Ned's reach. After Ned stretched for it, Kasey put the remote in his hand. She wrapped his fingers around it, just like she was trained to do.

Kasey repeated these steps with any object Ned asked her to get. In time, Kasey started bringing things to Ned's weaker right hand. She would tap them on his leg, make Ned reach, and then give him the object. Ellen couldn't believe her eyes. This little monkey was making Ned work a little harder every day. She was helping Ned get stronger.

Ellen called Megan to tell her what was happening. She asked if Megan had trained Kasey to do it.

"No, this wasn't part of Kasey's training. She's doing it on her own. But I'm not surprised."

"How can you not be surprised?" asked Ellen. "This is amazing!"

"Kasey is smart. She knows Ned and what he needs to get better."

Over and over, Kasey proved that she knew just what Ned needed. When Ned's body hurt, she crawled onto his chest. She wrapped her tail around his neck. She made deep cooing sounds. Her care made Ned feel better.

One day, Ned's hand slipped and hit the wheelchair controls. They got stuck on "go." The wheelchair crashed into a bed. It started racing toward a window. Kasey started screaming with all her might. She didn't stop until someone ran upstairs and stopped the runaway chair.

As Kasey and Ned's friendship grew, Ned's doctors saw changes in Ned. He had always worked hard to get stronger. But now he was healing faster.

"I think we can thank Kasey for how much better you are moving your arms," said one of Ned's therapists.

Kasey's ways of getting Ned to work harder were working. Ellen sensed that something else was happening, too. Ned wanted to take care of Kasey in return for all she did for him. He wanted to feed her, pet her, and hold her. For the first time since the accident, there was something Ned felt strongly about. He was responsible for Kasey.

When Kasey first came, Ned could hardly move from the neck down. He could barely move his hands. After five years with Kasey, Ned can move his hands, his arms, and his upper body. Ned can now hold Kasey. He can feed her walnuts. He can rub noses with her.

With Kasey at his side, Ned wants to tell the world his story. He and Kasey visit schools and hospitals. They tell kids to stay safe. They also tell them that no problem is too big. With help, you can be strong enough to get through anything.

"Kasey keeps me going. I will keep getting better. Kasey will take me further."

Don't Call Me a Pet

Kasey has made a big difference in Ned's life. When a monkey goes to Monkey College, it can be a big help to a person. But monkeys that haven't been to college are not good pets for humans. Monkeys are not like cats and dogs. They are wild animals, and wild animals can be dangerous. Visit your local zoo or wildlife center to learn more about monkeys.

RATS:
HEROES IN SMALL PACKAGES

This hero rat is doing a training exercise to find land mines.

African giant pouched rats have an incredible sense of smell that scientists are putting to good use.

Chapter 1

HIDDEN TALENT

Samo races through the tall grass. He keeps his nose to the ground, sniffing it carefully. He wears a harness attached to a long string. The grass is brown and Samo is brown, too. His handlers can hardly see him. They use the string to follow Samo's path. Suddenly Samo stops. He scratches at the ground. His handlers come up carefully behind him. Samo has found a hidden bomb called a land mine!

"Good job, Samo!" Samo's handler calls him back for his reward—a tasty piece of banana. Samo loves bananas. That's because he's an African giant pouched rat.

Bart Weetjens smiles proudly at the squirrel-size rat. He has worked very hard to bring his rats to this African minefield. Bart remembers how just 15 years ago, people laughed at his idea to use rats to find land mines. After all, who would believe that rats could be useful working animals? They aren't strong and fast like a horse, or brave and loyal like a dog. They don't have abilities like dolphins, which are sometimes trained to find bombs underwater. But rats are pretty special. They are smart and easy to train. They don't mind doing simple tasks over and over. And they have a great sense of smell.

Most people see rats as a pest. But Bart saw something great: the chance to solve a global problem—land mines. Millions of land mines are hidden on or under the ground in nearly 80 countries around the world. That's more than one in every three countries. The bombs are left over from wars. Sometimes they are hard to see when they are covered by a thin layer of dirt or grass. If someone steps on a mine, it can explode. The devices cause thousands of injuries and deaths every year.

Bart knew that people could never be safe with such deadly weapons around. The land mines had to go. But how? Finding land mines is dangerous and difficult. Many people have tried different ways to do it. Each method has problems. What could Bart try that hadn't been done before? To find an answer, Bart thought back to his childhood in Belgium and a little hamster named Goldy, who started his love for rodents.

"Happy birthday, Bart!"

Bart's mom and dad had opened the door to his room. His dad carried a small cage wrapped in ribbon.

"What's this?" Bart shouted, running to the cage.

A shaggy-haired hamster poked his head out. Bart reached in and scooped up the golden ball of fur.

"Wow, he's so soft and cute. I'll name him Goldy after the color of his hair. Thanks, Mom and Dad!"

"You have to take care of him yourself, Bart," said Bart's mom.

"That's right," agreed his dad. "Goldy is your responsibility."

"I promise I will. You won't have to worry about a thing."

Bart kept his promise to his parents and took care of Goldy's every need. The two were never apart. Bart kept Goldy in the pocket of his shirt. Sometimes, Goldy snoozed in the crook of his arm. Bart took Goldy along when he went to play with his friends. He and Goldy went shopping in the supermarket. He even took Goldy to school!

No one knows I have a hamster hidden in my clothes, Bart thought to himself. It was like he and Goldy shared a secret.

It wasn't long before Bart's secret got out. Bart was in trouble.

"Bart, I'm glad that you and Goldy are so close. But you can't take him out of the house. It's not safe for him," Bart's mom told him. She knew that if Goldy got away, the little fur ball would be really hard to find.

Bart agreed to leave Goldy at home from then on. But he worried that his buddy would get lonely. Bart wondered if he could get a friend for Goldy. His parents said he could. Soon after the

Did You Know?

African giant rats have pouches in their cheeks like hamsters that they use to store food.

new hamster came, baby hamsters were born.

Bart's parents didn't want a dozen little Goldys running around the house. They told Bart he would have to find a new home for the babies once they were big enough to leave their mom.

Bart took the young hamsters to a pet store. To his surprise, the shopkeeper gave him some money for each hamster.

This is great! thought Bart. *If Goldy has more babies, I can have fun and make money, too!*

The shopkeeper said Bart could also sell him other baby animals. Before long, a row of cages lined a wall of Bart's room. Inside, hamsters, gerbils, squirrels, and rats ran around happily.

Bart's parents were a little nervous about having so many rodents in the house. But Bart cleaned the animals' cages. He gave his rodents fresh food and water every day. He played with them and petted them. Since the hobby made their son so happy, Bart's parents allowed it.

Rats became Bart's favorite of all. They were so smart and friendly! Plus, they had an amazing sense of smell.

I bet rats could do lots of cool things, Bart thought.

At age 14, Bart left home to go to boarding school. He had to leave his rodent friends behind. Little did Bart know that when he grew up, rats would be part of his life again. This time, the stakes would be higher. Bart was going to use rats to save lives.

Giant Rats

African giant pouched rats can be found in many parts of Africa. They weigh 2 to 3 pounds (0.9 to 1.4 kg) and can grow up to 3 feet (0.9 m) long (including their tail). In the wild, they're active at night and sleep during the day.

While this type of rat is social and easy to train, they don't make very good pets. The animals have a strong chewing instinct. They'll chew on anything they find in your house.

Land mines like this one are a very serious problem all over the world.

Chapter 2

AN EXPLOSIVE PROBLEM

It was 1995. A war had ended in Mozambique, a country in Africa. Both sides had used land mines. They buried the small bombs under dirt or leaves. When a person stepped on one of the mines, it would blow up. When a car ran over one, it would explode. Some mines were buried to keep the enemy away. Others were used to scare the enemy.

When the war was over, the killing stopped, right? No, it didn't. The mines were still there. People stepped on them and were hurt or killed. Farmers ran over them while plowing their fields. Kids stepped on them when playing ball.

Mozambique is not the only country with land mines. About 100 million mines are buried all over the world. They kill or hurt thousands of people each year. This is a very big problem.

Since the war ended, many countries have agreed to stop using land mines. They have also agreed to get rid of the land mines they have. But there is still one big problem: How do you get rid of the land mines that are already buried in the ground?

Many people have tried to solve this problem but have not been successful. This is mostly because finding the land mines is dangerous and very expensive. The problem had gotten so bad that people were beginning to lose hope.

Bart knew all of this, and he wanted to help. He read what other people had written about finding land mines. Many people had ideas on how to get rid of mines. One group used a high-tech sensor to find them. Another made a machine that could see mines in the dirt. These ideas didn't work very well. They needed electricity, and mines are often in places that don't have electricity.

Other people had made special cars. These cars had armor to keep them safe when a mine exploded. But they only worked on flat land. Metal detectors weren't right either. They found every piece of metal on the ground. They found some mines, but they found mostly coins and rusty screws.

Dogs were trained to sniff out TNT, the stuff that makes land mines explode. But sometimes the dog would set off the bomb and be hurt or killed. No one wants a dog to be hurt. The dogs got sick a lot, too. People realized this idea wasn't a good solution either.

Bart needed a new way to find land mines quickly and well. He knew that it had to be simple and not cost a lot of money. One day, he read an article about scientists who trained gerbils to find bombs. He thought back to the rats he had kept as pets when he was young. They were smarter than gerbils, and they had a great sense of smell. *That's it!* he thought. The idea struck him like a lightning bolt.

Rats can do that! I'll train African rats to sniff out mines. They're too small to explode the mines because they don't weigh enough. Their lives won't be at risk. Plus, they don't cost too much to feed. They can't get sick from local diseases because they are already used to them. And they are easy to take wherever they need to go.

Bart typed a letter. He sent it to a group that gives money to projects that help the world. The group told him they didn't like his idea. They didn't give him any money. Bart sent the letter to another group and then another. Almost two years passed, and still no group thought Bart's idea would work.

Finally, in 1997, someone liked his idea. The Belgian government gave him the money he needed to test it. Bart set up a training program. He had to make his rats ready for the hard work in the minefields. Only then could Bart's rats become the heroes he hoped they would be.

Bart chose the African giant pouched rat for his project. These rats live an average of six to eight years. They're calm, friendly, and easy to handle. Plus, with their large size, they're easier to spot in thick grass than smaller rats.

Bart got the idea to use the pouched rat from a friend. When his friend was in Africa, he saw a person walking one on a leash.

This is the rat for us! Bart thought when he found out about it.

Bart's training program starts soon after the rats are born. At five weeks old, the rats are ready to leave their mother. People take care of them for one to two weeks so the rats get used to being around humans. Each rat is given a name. Then, it's time to start the training.

The rat trainers teach the rats to do simple tricks. When a rat does a good job, the trainer gives it a food treat. At the same time, the trainer makes a clicking sound. The rat learns that a click means it has done a good job and will get a treat.

The trainers teach the rats to find TNT by its smell. At "sniff school," rats go into a large tank with slots along the bottom. Scents are loaded into the slots.

A rat runs along the bottom of the tank, its nose to the ground. When it stops at the TNT scent, CLICK . . . Snack time! The rat gets a bit of banana or a peanut each time it finds the TNT smell.

The training is repeated until the rats learn to stop and scratch at the spot where they smell TNT. From start to finish, the training program takes from eight to twelve months. Some rats learn fast and some learn slowly. Bart's rats seemed to be getting the hang of it pretty quickly.

Rat Athletes

Talk about a rat race! At a college in Nebraska, rats compete in events like the long jump, tightrope walk, rope climb, and weight lifting. It's like the Olympic Games for rats!

Students train the rats as part of a science class. When the rats learn a step to a trick, they're rewarded with goodies like protein pellets or yogurt chips. Eventually, the behaviors are combined into a complete skill.

A rat is rewarded with a chunk of banana for a job well done.

Chapter 3

RATS TO THE RESCUE

Bart's rats practiced for months until they were expert TNT finders. Bart knew that they were ready for the next step: It was time to go outside. Bart set up a fake minefield. He buried old mines that were fixed so they couldn't explode. The mines still had bits of TNT for the rats to sniff out. They were great for the rats to practice on.

Pouched rats aren't used to being in the sun. They usually only come out at night. Bart made sure to protect them. The scientists put sunscreen in the rats' ears.

The rats scampered over the grass. They found all the TNT smells. Bart knew they were ready to be heroes. Now it was time for them to find real land mines. In 2008 and 2009, Bart's company, HeroRats, sent 30 rats to sniff more than 600 square miles (1,500 sq km) of land in Mozambique. The rats found 400 land mines! They did such a good job that they got a new goal. The government asked HeroRats to find all the land mines in the country by 2014.

Bart knew his rats could do it. Every day, he sees how the rats have helped people.

In 2010, HeroRats was sent to a village where the electric company couldn't work. There were mines hidden where they needed to put wires. Many people had no electricity for cooking or refrigeration. Children couldn't study at night because they didn't have lights. They couldn't use electronics like computers or televisions.

Bart's HeroRats found 40 mines in the small minefield. A team came to destroy the mines. The area was safe for the electric company workers.

When Bart visited the village later, he saw how much it had changed. Now the village had electricity. There were new schools, stores, and places for people to work. The villagers had a better life—and it was all thanks to HeroRats.

Meet the Rats

Each HeroRat has its own name and personality. Here are a few of the program's most famous critters.

ANZO

Bart's favorite rat lived to be nine years old. That's very, very old for a rat. She had so many babies that lots of today's HeroRats are Anzo's grandchildren and great-grandchildren.

ARARAT

Ararat was
HeroRats' star student.
He breezed through the
training program. Bart sent
him to Mozambique right away. If there's
a land mine around, Ararat will find it.

GRIGORY

Grigory isn't a top student, but he tries
hard. During his field training,
he missed a fake mine.
But Grigory's trainer
isn't ready to give up
on him. "Tomorrow,
he'll know he needs
to do better."

At another village, mines had been buried in a field next to a school. Teachers and students feared that one step could bring disaster. Children could not go outside at recess. They had to be careful on their way home from school.

The HeroRats were called in to sniff out the land mines. They cleared the whole area—finding more than 100 mines! Now, children can play safely in the schoolyard. They can have recess and play soccer and tag.

Bart and his rats have come a long way. They are still working in Mozambique. Now they clear land mines in neighboring Tanzania too. The group is planning to go to Thailand, a country in Asia where many mines are buried. They're also beginning another important job.

Some scientists thought that if these rats were so good at finding bombs, they might be good at finding other things too. As luck would have it, they are. These rats are now finding an illness called tuberculosis (sounds like TOO-BURR-CUE-LOW-SIS).

Tuberculosis, also called TB, mostly attacks people's lungs. It is a big problem all over the world. When someone has TB, he or she can give it to other people by sneezing or coughing.

Did You Know?

Rats are not the only animals that can sniff for deadly disease. Some dogs have been trained to find cancer using their sense of smell.

In the United States, TB is not very common. In Africa, many people have this illness. In many cases, it can be deadly.

The good news is that there is medicine to treat people with TB. The bad news is that it costs a lot of money to test people for the disease. But HeroRats can help! When a person has TB, a certain kind of germ is found in their spit. The germ has a scent. And as Bart's rats have proved, rats are very good at picking out scents.

Scientists started training the HeroRats to sniff for the TB germ. They did this the same way they trained the rats to sniff for land mines. They put different samples of spit into a tank with holes in the bottom. The rats would wander over the holes. When they smelled the TB scent, they would stop for a few seconds. If they were correct, they received a banana or a peanut. Pretty soon the rats learned to pass by the holes where they didn't smell TB. They went straight for the holes that smelled like the germ—and got the reward!

Once the rats were trained, doctors put them to the test. They found out that the rats aren't just as good as expensive tests—they're even better! They find almost twice as many TB cases as the tests do.

The testing with rats is still in the beginning stages. Scientists have more work to do before the test can be used on real people. Still, they are hopeful that the rats could one day be the number one test for TB. If the rats are as good at finding the illness as some people think they are, they may save a lot of lives.

HeroRats is not alone in working to solve the problems of land mines or tuberculosis. Many people around the world are helping, and it is paying off. In 2002, almost 12,000 people around the world were killed or hurt in land mine accidents. Now, that number is less than 4,200 a year. In 2011, the number of TB cases went down for the first time in years.

Bart knows there is still work to do. But with his rats' help, the world is already a better place.

THE END

DON'T MISS!

**Turn the page
for a sneak preview . . .**

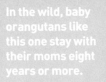

In the wild, baby orangutans like this one stay with their moms eight years or more.

Chapter 1

A SCAMP IS BORN

July 1965, Omaha, Nebraska

A young orangutan peers out of his cage at the Henry Doorly Zoo. No humans are in sight. The coast is clear.

He sticks his long fingers through the chain-link fence. He bends back one corner. He pulls. *ZZIIIIP!* The stiff metal fencing unravels like a hand-knit scarf.

Some time later, veterinarian Lee Simmons arrives at work. He rounds a bend in the path and *yikes!* Dr. Simmons stops in his tracks. It couldn't be, but it is. A shaggy, red-haired ape sits up in a tree. *How did he get loose?*

The ape is about six years old, tailless, and weighs 100 pounds (45 kg). He has a mustache and beard like a famous movie character. For that reason he is called Fu Manchu. Fu's arms are super strong and longer than most fourth graders are tall. In a wrestling match against a man, the orangutan would win.

The ape doesn't move or make a sound. But Dr. Simmons sees a twinkle in his eyes. The vet can't help but wonder if Fu knew what he was doing. *It's like he's been sitting there just waiting for me.*

Fu climbs down. The sun sparkles on his red hair as he scrambles back to his cage. Dr. Simmons follows, shaking his head. *What a crazy ape!* He locks Fu inside. He calls someone to fix the fence and then goes about his normal business. And Fu goes about his—dreaming up more hijinks to come.

Fu was born in a rain forest on the Indonesian island of Sumatra (sounds like SUE-MAH-TRA). Like most baby orangutans, Fu probably never knew his father. Orangutan mothers care for their helpless babies. Fu's mother nursed him. She held him and snuggled him. Every night she built them a nest high in the treetops.

These sleeping nests were the size of

Did You Know?

For the first few weeks after they're born, baby orangutans cling to their moms' bellies.

bathtubs. Fu's mother made them by twisting leafy branches together. Each fresh, new nest must have felt as comfy to Fu as clean bedsheets do to you.

Usually Fu and his mom stayed dry in their cozy bed in the sky. At other times thunder boomed. Rain fell in sheets. Then the apes huddled together and turned giant leaves into umbrellas.

During the day, Fu often rode on his mother's back. He clutched her hair as they swung through the trees looking for durian (sounds like DUR-EE-ANN) fruits. Durian fruits stink like sweaty gym socks. But orangutans go ape for the smelly stuff.

The problem is durian fruits don't all

ripen at the same time, and the trees are scattered. To find them, orangutans must keep a map of the forest inside their heads. For Fu's mother it must have been like memorizing a school bus route with hundreds of stops.

Finding water was easier. It collects in hollow tree trunks after a rain. Fu might have gotten a drink by scooping water out with a folded leaf. Or maybe he chewed leaves into a sort of sponge. Then he sopped up water and dripped it into his mouth. Either way, Fu used leaves as tools.

Long ago, Indonesian people dubbed these clever apes "orangutans." In their language the word *orang* means

Did You Know?

As baby orangutans get older, they ride "piggyback" to get a better view of their surroundings.

"person" and *utan* means "forest."
Together you get "person of the forest."

One day Fu and his mother heard
strange sounds in the swamp. Hunters had
entered the jungle. They carried axes and
homemade nets on their backs. Rivers of
sweat ran down the men's bare chests.
Armies of insects buzzed in their faces.
But nothing stopped them. The men
were animal collectors. They feed their
families by catching and selling wild
animals. A baby orangutan will get them
a lot of money.

Did Fu's mother know they wanted her
baby? Probably not, but she sensed danger.
She swung from limb to limb, snapping off
branches. She threw the branches down on
the hunters.

The animal collectors looked up. The mother ape looked like a tiny black doll hanging against the blue sky. Was she holding a baby?

The hunters had a traditional way of catching orangutans. They didn't try to climb up after them. Not at first. That might have spooked the ape into escaping through the treetops. Instead, the animal collectors formed a circle. They pulled out their axes and hacked away at tree trunks.

The ground shook as a tall tree crashed to the forest floor. Then a second one, and a third. The trees were so close together that each one that fell knocked down another. CHOP! CHOP! The men worked their way to the last tree—the one holding the apes.

Want to know what happens next? Be sure to check out *Ape Escapes!* Available wherever books and ebooks are sold.

INDEX

Boldface indicates illustrations.

African giant pouched rats
    cheek pouches 76
    chewing instinct 79
    eyesight 84
    sense of smell 70, 73, 84
    size 72, 79, 86
Animal collectors 108–109
Avalanche rescue dogs 23, **23**

Baleen whales **12,** 13
Bike helmets 45, **45**

Capuchin monkeys
    fingers and toes 50
    intelligence 53, 57
    jumping ability 61
    life span 53
    size 53
Cetaceans 12

Dogs
    dolphin rescue **16,** 17–25,
      26, 27–35
    home helpers 44
    as pets 23
    sense of smell 20–21
    TNT detection 84
    whale-poop detection 33
    working dogs 23, **23**
Dolphins

blowholes 10–11
    intelligence 9
    stranded **6,** 7–11, 27–32
    teeth 12, 13
    whistles 9, 10

Hamsters 74–77
HeroRats 92–93, **94–95,** 96, 98,
    100

K-9 units 25

Labrador retrievers **4–5, 16,** 18,
    19, **26**
Land mines 68, 72–74, **80,**
    81–86, 91–96, 98, 100

Mozambique 81–82, 92, 95, 96

Orangutans **102,** 103–109

Rat athletes 89, **89**

TNT 84, 88, 91, 92
Toothed whales 12, **12,** 13
Tuberculosis (TB) 97–100

Whales
    stranded 6, 8, 15, 32
    study of 33
    types of **12,** 12–13

MORE INFORMATION

To find more information about the animal species featured in this book, check out these books and websites:

Face to Face With Dolphins,
National Geographic, 2007

National Geographic Kids Everything Dolphins,
National Geographic, 2012

Rain Forest Alliance "Kid's Corner: Capuchin Monkey"
www.rainforest-alliance.org/kids/species-profiles/capuchin-monkey

National Geographic Digital Motion Rat Genius (video)
www.natgeoeducationvideo.com/film/283/rat-genius

National Geographic Channel "Capuchin Monkey" (short video)
natgeotv.com.au/videos/animals/capuchin-monkey-CF3958F9.aspx

This book is dedicated to the human heroes: Ned Sullivan, Chris Blankenship, and Bart Weetjens. Thank you for sharing your inspiring stories and making our world a better place.

CREDITS

Cover, Bill Sumner; 4, Jason Nuttle; 6, Tony Ashby/AFP/Getty Images; 12 (LE), Flukeprint/Dreamstime; 12 (RT), Shawn Jackson/Dreamstime; 16, Jason Nuttle; 23, Amidala76/Shutterstock ; 26, Bill Sumner; 33, New England Aquarium; 36, Ivan de Petrovski; 38, Courtesy of Ellen Rogers; 45, Osebeck/Dreamstime; 48, Courtesy of Ellen Rogers; 57, Vilainecrevette/Dreamstime; 58, Courtesy of Ellen Rogers; 67, Courtesy of Ellen Rogers; 68, Stuart Franklin/Magnum Photos; 70, Alvaro Laiz; 79, David Rengel; 80, Stuart Franklin/Magnum Photos; 89, William Lauer/Lincoln Journal Star; 90, Stuart Franklin/Magnum Photos; 94, Alvaro Laiz; 95 (UP), Lieve Blancquaert; 95 (LO), APOPO; 101, Cyril Ruoso; 102, Life on White/Alamy; 102 (background), Elena Elisseeva/Dreamstime; 111, Shawn Jackson/Dreamstime

ACKNOWLEDGMENTS

Elizabeth Carney would like to acknowledge the following organizations for helping to make this book possible:

APOPO and HeroRats
www.apopo.org

The Dolphin and Marine Medical Research Foundation
www.dmmr.org

Helping Hands
www.monkeyhelpers.org